# HOW TO WIN AT FINANCES.

## Increasing Financial Knowledge to Develop a Winning Approach to Money

Randolph Solomon MBA, AAMS
Tyler Woodall, CLCS

# CONTENTS

Title Page

Copyright

About the Authors   1

The Origin of the US Dollar   3

The Value of Money   5

How Do Banks Help with Money?   7

How Does the Government Control Our Money?   9

The Stock Market   12

Types of Financial Products   14

Investing in Real Estate   24

Retirement Vehicles   29

Life Insurance   37

Developing a Plan   43

How to Win at Finances   53

# ABOUT THE AUTHORS

Asset management specialist, Randolph Solomon is a dedicated consultant in all aspects of investing. Specializing in businesses, real estate, and alternative investing, his mission lies with helping others achieve financial freedom by increasing their financial knowledge and providing individualized planning and care. Holding his MBA, Randolph also provides strategic business consultations to assist with organizational development and sustainable growth. He is a broker associate of McCoy Wright Commercial Real Estate and a partner of The Win Agency.

Tyler Woodall is a commercial risk advisor, working with small and medium sized businesses to find creative solutions to managing their risks. This takes place in the form of insurance (commercial general liability, workers compensation, cyber insurance, etc.), as well as through advising and teaching about other financial principles and methods. Tyler has earned his CLCS designation (Commercial Lines Coverage Specialist) in an effort to further his expertise and available resources for business owners.

## Contact Information

Randolph Solomon MBA, AAMS
McCoy Wright Commercial Real Estate/ The Win Agency
randy@mccoywright.com / randy@winatfinances.com
(843) 624 - 8152

Tyler Woodall CLCS
The WIN Agency
tyler@winatfinances.com
(864) 934 - 6985

# THE ORIGIN OF THE US DOLLAR

*"You either master money, or, on some level, money masters you."* — ***Tony Robbins***

The United States of America. A country forged in revolution and war, American civilization at its core exemplifies the characteristics of resilience, determination, and power. Led by General George Washington, the United States started its journey to dominance in 1776 following its victory in the revolutionary war against Great Britain. In order to fund such rapid growth and develop an entity separate from its European roots, the US depended heavily on funding wherever possible, prior to the creation of the Dollar the US utilized Continental currency. Due to the discrepancies between financial institutions and the ease of which this currency was counterfeited, Congress made the decision to charter the Bank of North America, in Philadelphia, to serve as a centralized institution to provide stabilization for the dollar and coordinate business with, and for, the government.

It is important to recognize how, even in the earliest stage of the US monetary system, the knowledge and mastery of money created strategic superiority. Let's take a look at how in this time of economic turmoil, finance was utilized to sustain the monetary system of the United States. Renowned financier Robert Morris, who at the time served as the congressional superintendent of the Finance for the United states, was tasked with chartering and leading the Bank of North America during a time of war and economic crime, by which the early confederation was surely facing bankruptcy. With only 99 subscribers to the National Bank shares, Morris funded the bank with a $450,000 loan from Congress in French silver, which was then utilized to loan back to congress. As congress faced economic travels the bank then sold the governments shares to repay the bank, and subsequently relent the money back to Congress to keep it afloat.

Shortly thereafter through the Coinage Act of 1792, coinage was introduced into the currency system to create a more organized monetary system, making the US the first country in the world to utilize a decimal system for their currency. Following this systematic implementation, the US formed more than 1,500 private banking institutions, all of which were permitted to print and utilize their own state approved paper currencies. Naturally, within the following few decades there were thousands of variations of these state level bank notes and with the Civil War looming over the country, the government passed the Act of 1861 and the Treasury Act of 1863.

The Act of 1861 allowed the US to introduce paperbacks into their national currency in addition to their coinage system. This currency, " The Greenback", now known as the US Dollar, was to be regulated and identified throughout the states. The Treasury Act of 1863 allowed the United States to start forming its own national level banks. These banks were designed to help fund the war, by establishing homes for the national currency, and support by the government, this allowed them to purchase more bonds, government securities, and issue more money on a national level; a saving grace for the young US economy stressed by the Civil War.

Following the end of the Civil War in 1865 and a few years of recovery and restructure, the US enacted the Federal Reserve Act of 1913. This act created one centralized bank and banking system to be utilized uniformly throughout the entire country, the system that has over time grown into what you and I use on a daily basis!

# THE VALUE OF MONEY

*"If we command our wealth, we shall be rich and free. If our wealth commands us, we are poor indeed."* — **Edmund Burke**

Money can be identified as anything that can be utilized as a means of payment in exchange for any type of goods or services or to repay any debts. The United State's form of money, the US Dollar, gives us as American citizens a uniform medium of exchange to utilize in our daily transactions and debt settlements. This same concept is emulated throughout most countries throughout the world, and that is why each country has their own unique currency. That is their preferred medium of exchange. For example, in Japan they use the Yen (¥), and in Europe, the Euro (€).

When it comes to understanding money, how it works, and ultimately how to make it work for you. One of the key principles that one must understand is the concept of inflation. Most people have experienced inflation at some point in their lives and probably never noticed it. Have you ever noticed how as time passes the same things become more and more expensive? Whether that's groceries, or gas, or modern luxury items. Inflation is the economic principle that represents the decline in the value of money, which subsequently causes things to increase in price. One clear example of this is just the cost of a loaf of bread. The fact that in 2008 a single loaf of Sara Lee bread cost $1.68, but in 2020 the same loaf of bread costs $2.08. That's a 19% increase in price over 12 years. How about gas prices? Any driver in the US has bared witness to the gross increase in prices, even in the previous 5 years.

Let's take a moment to consider this realistic scenario: If money is declining in value year by year, which is subsequently causing things to increase in price year by year, then how are we going to afford our cost of living if we make the same amount of money every year for the rest of our lives? Or, even if we make the same amount of money for 5 years before we reach a promotion, that still causes issues. It's a scary reality. A scarier reality is when you step back and consider retirement. If we are funding retirement plans with post tax dollars, and not putting any thought or consideration to the security and performance of those investments, do you really think you'll have enough to keep up with this increased cost of living? College. Cars. Houses. All of these life necessities are influenced by this general economic principle. So how do we as American's take the money we are making today and grow it to where we can afford to live tomorrow?

# HOW DO BANKS HELP
# WITH MONEY?

*"In the simplest sense, the key to the performance of any traditional commercial bank ... is the profitability of the loans it makes."* — **Robert Wilmers, Chairman and CEO of M&T Bank**

Every adult, whether young or old, has at some point gone to the bank and opened an account. A checking account, savings account, business account, maybe gone to take out a mortgage/car loan, purchased a CD in hopes of making a "sound" investment. But let's take some time to learn more about banks, what they do for you, what the government uses them for, and how they fit into the overall financial profile.

As we learned in the earlier chapter, banks were originally instilled at the state level, then national, and now an established central institution. But what most people don't realize is that banks are the life source connecting the US Citizens' hard earned money back to the government. Now don't get us wrong, banks serve a great benefit to us as citizens. Without a bank, where would we store our money? Where would we get loans for our life necessities? What would life be without loans and debit/credit cards? But in order for us to understand money and how we can make it work for us, we must understand how Banks work.

When we go to the bank and open our first bank account, typically a checking account, we deposit that money in cash into our account, where we literally never physically see it again. So what happens to that money? The bank takes your deposit and pools it into a much bigger pool of money that they then utilize to distribute the loans, mortgages, and credit that we all get to enjoy. In this simplest form we see how the banks use our money, and make it work for them. And how does the bank make money in this situation? Well that's simple. The money the banks take in deposits from it's customers. The basis of the loans that are distributed back to the customers are essentially from the customer's money, and the interest that the banks charge the customer's on the money that is lent, is where the bank wins. We see this clear cycle of money from clients, to bank, back to client, then even more back to the bank.

# HOW DOES THE GOVERNMENT CONTROL OUR MONEY?

*" The issue is always the same: the government or the market. There is no third solution." —**Ludwig Von Mises***

Although the banking process may be eye opening to many reading this, it is a necessary evil, as loans, mortgages, and overall credit are a critical aspect in maintaining the current economy. Considering this direct connection between the Banking system and the economy, the next question in most people's mind is how does the government get involved with the bank? In terms of the US Economy, one could consider money to be the blood that pumps and circulates throughout the economy (the body) to power and operate all the functions and departments (organs, limbs) necessary for the country to run. So where's the heart? The beating heart of the US economy is the Central Bank. In the US, this Central Bank is known as the Federal Reserve, and each country throughout the world has their own unique Central Bank.

Very similar to the human body, the more money (blood) that circulates throughout the economy, the better the performance. When the economy has a large supply of free flowing money this means that banks are able to distribute loans and finances easier than normal. As a result, this  influx of cash subsequently allows the large companies to be able to afford more and expand their business, banks can charge higher interest rates because people have more money, and overall unemployment lowers because the business expansion opens a larger number of jobs and opportunities for people.

**Print Money**

Many people think about the concept of money and how it is printed and contemplate, " Why can't the government simply print more money to meet our needs?" the flaw to this logic is simple. The Federal Reserve can physically print as much money as it wants to, yes. But a direct result of printing more money, with the same level of production and success in the economy results in a simply watered-down dollar. The less the dollar is worth, the more money people have to physically make to afford their cost of living, and that. Is inflation.

## Altering Reserve Requirements

An effective alternative to this inflationary money tactic is the Federal Reserve's ability to control the reserve requirements of commercial banks. What that means is that the government can regulate how much of our money the bank is able to leverage and redistribute as a loan. The lower the reserve requirement, the more of our money the bank has to distribute and create loans. For example, if the federal reserve sets the reserve requirement to 10%, and the bank has a total of $10 million dollars in deposited money, that means it must keep $1 million dollars of this money stored in their vault, and they are free to issue the other $9 million dollars back into the economy as loans. This ability to open and close the flow of money through the commercial banking system allows the government to control the access to loans, credit, and financing to the public.

## Influencing Interest Rates

Obviously based on what has been covered up to this point, it is fully known that the US commercial banks generate their profits from the interest rates they issue on the money we store with them. The clear question is "Who sets that level of interest?", a very sound question to ask indeed. Most banks are able to compete in the banking world by offering more affordable interest rates, this is possible because the federal reserve does not have the power to directly set the interest rates. Although the Fed can't set a specific interest rate for banks to use when distributing loans to people, they are able to utilize their control over the amount of reserve money and the amount of interest the federal reserve is able to charge to commercial banks for money, they can subsequently influence the rates that commercial banks charge to their customers.

The Federal Reserve not only serves as a guide for the commercial banking world, they also serve as a source of loans for the banks themselves. Banks are able to loan money from the Federal Reserve to maintain operations and increase business, this rate is called the federal discount rate. This discount rate has an influence on the banks ability to re-lend this money to customers. For example if the discount rate is lower for the bank, then they are able to establish loans at a lower interest rate to their customers, which means more money can circulate through the economy. On the other hand, if the Fed chooses to raise the discount rate, it will subsequently tighten the economic money supply because the banks have to raise their interest rates which mean people take less loans and the money supply lowers.

### Open Market Operations

As seen through our increased understanding of the origins of money, the economy has utilized government securities to influence the flow of money in the economy since its inception. How this works, is that the Federal Reserve will buy government securities from commercial banks to infuse capital back into the economy and subsequently lower the commercial bank's interest rates because they have more money to lend. On the other hand, if the Fed dictated that the money supply needed to slow, it would sell Government Securities back to the banks to lower their available capital and subsequently increase interest rates to their customers, and get closer to the Fed's desired discount rate.

# THE STOCK MARKET

*"Rule number one: Don't lose money. Rule number two: Don't forget rule number one."* — **Warren Buffett**

Most people reading this book, or who have come across investing conversation in the past are familiar with two key terms. The New York Stock Exchange (NYSE) and Wall Street. Although infamous in and of itself, contrary to most people's belief, the NYSE is not the first Securities Exchange in the US. The honor of the first Securities Exchange in the US is held by the Philadelphia Stock Exchange which was formed in 1790. The world-renowned New York Stock exchange was forged two short years after by 24 stock brokers under a buttonwood tree on Wall Street, 2 Decades later the exchange had grown in size and stature and was officially recognized as the New York Stock Exchange. At the epicenter, the NYSE served as a catalyst for financial operations within New York and the United States and led the way for New York becoming the new financial center of the country. It is important to note that the stock market is not solely represented by wall street or the NYSE, these are merely facilities to conduct trading/exchanges of stocks.

Companies caught wind of the power of the market and the benefit of becoming "public" which has set the standard for large companies to get their companies on this exchange/ in the market. Companies are able to utilize these exchanges to raise capital for their businesses to fuel their growth and expansion. If a company is needing money and wants to grow, they divvy up the value of their organization into equal amounts (shares) which they sell publicly on these exchanges, and in exchange for receiving the capital from these investors buying the shares, the investors subsequently own a portion of the company (becoming shareholders). This simple concept is why companies become more popular and generate more revenue when their stock prices rise. In combination with this, most large companies that expand to the market offer incentives for people to purchase their shares, called dividends. If companies generate enough profit per year they will elect to offer dividends to their shareholders, often in hopes of increasing the buying incentive of the public. These dividends are additional returns that companies pay out to investors, some paying quarterly or annually.

Although most people are not aware of this mutual dependency, the stock market serves as an active tool to open companies to the public. The stock market breaks out into multiple indexes (groups) to categorize certain groups of companies including: The S&P 500, the Nasdaq, Dow Jones, just to name a few. The S&P 500 is the most recognized of these indexes, it measures the value of the 500 largest companies that are listed on the New York Stock Exchange, as well as another index called the Nasdaq, based on their market capitalization (total market value of a company's sellable shares).

Decades of ups and downs, infamous brokers, crashes, and legislation has developed the stock market into this almost autonomous resource we all have come to know and utilize on our path to wealth.

# TYPES OF FINANCIAL PRODUCTS

*"The secret to investing is to figure out the value of something– and then pay a lot less."* —*Joel Greenblatt*

### Stocks

Stocks could be considered the most common form of financial investment. At its core a stock is simply a representation of a piece of ownership of a company. As a company grows and expands in size, in order to promote themselves and receive economic support, a company will "offer" their company to the public by divvying up their overall company value into X amount of shares. These shares provide the company with additional revenue that can be used to increase production and profitability of the company, which in terms makes the stocks (ownership) more valuable as well! As this economic value (profit) increases, companies make their stock more appealing by offering dividends. These dividends represent a percentage of the company's overall profit that they are willing to distribute back to their shareholders (owners).

### Bonds

We've covered how stocks represent proportionate ownership of a large company in order to help the company expand and fund their growth. On the other hand, bonds represent providing debt (lending money) to a business or government entity and their respective subsidiaries. We have all driven around our local cities and seen a number of construction projects, local monuments or venues, improvements and buildings. All of these add value and character to our hometowns or favorite vacation spot, but have you ever wondered how these projects are funded? Any tax paying American citizen is going to immediately implicate Uncle Sam, who in fact, is not entirely guilty in providing funding to these projects. But these government entities have more than just taxes to fuel their goals, they offer bonds to the public.

The same way that stocks offer normal people the opportunity to own "a part" of a company; bonds enable investors to serve a role in improving certain government/business projects by loaning money with the promise of repayment. Bonds typically have a set value of par ($1000) so businesses/government entities will present investors with little to low risk investment opportunities by offering these bonds at a discount to that par price (for example $900). This effective strategy enables a business/government entity to say " Hey! We're building a new water treatment facility here in (XYZ city) and need your help funding the project! You can purchase our bonds at $900 and receive par value in (x) years following the project's completion!" Now some may be thinking, what's the point of putting money away for X amount of years for a couple hundred bucks profit, but one of the best benefits of bonds is the guaranteed dividend payment.

This dividend payment is a set interest rate (coupon rate ) of the par value ($1000) of the bond, which is broken up and paid on a quarterly basis. For example a discount bond selling at $900 paying a 5% coupon rate with a 20 year maturity would get paid ( ($1000 * .05) /4) = $50 annual payment per year ($12.50 per quarter) for 20 year totalling an $1100 profit at maturity. ($1000 dividend profit over 20 years - $900 bond payment + $1000 par repayment). Another substantial benefit of bonds are the taxation, bonds enable an investor to receive tax free income over the course of the bonds life, so High Net Worth investors that are able to put away a substantial portion of their revenue towards these bonds (either individually or through a fund) are able to receive substantial tax free income with lump sum payment throughout their later years.

### Mutual Funds
When it comes to investing, one of the most important

elements of establishing wealth and long-term success lies in the diversification of your investment. This means that when economic events affect one element of your portfolio (group of investments), whether that's by category (stocks or bonds) or individual investments, they can be negated by the adverse response by a different investment. For example, if the Tech industry takes a substantial hit, having stocks in energy or another sector that responds positively to negative tech events would essentially balance out the portfolio from substantial loss.

Mutual funds enable investors to invest their money into structured portfolios of diversified stocks in different industries, or compositions, without having to buy the amount of individual shares that would comprise the same portfolio (which can be thousands of dollars for a well developed portfolio). In exchange, investors don't own the entire shares within the portfolio, they own a respective portion of the fund rather than the physical stock and share this ownership with all the other investors in the fund. Certain funds even offer dividends with fund investment, as well.

A rule of thumb, most funds or structured products seek returns comparable to the S&P 500 that we covered earlier. The performance of these top tier 500 companies virtually reflect the overall performance of the financial markets, so anything close to that level of return could be considered an extremely attractive investment. One of the drawbacks of these funds is that you have to pay for their performance. These funds are actively managed by analysts and fund managers, which means they do come with a range of fees. These fees can occur at the front end, back end, or throughout the term of investment.

### Exchange Traded Funds (ETF)

ETFs are very similar to mutual funds in that they are a diversified portfolio of stocks that enable investors to diversify, without having to pay for the portfolio composition themselves.

Also, like mutual funds, these ETFs do have the ability to provide dividends based on the stock composition. The primary difference between these funds and mutual funds is that these can be actively traded on an exchange. Mutual funds are traded once a day and performance is dictated by day by day in that way, as to where ETFs are traded like stocks throughout the day and offer the investor to buy, trade, and sell more frequently and effectively. In addition to this, ETF's are more tax efficient in comparison to mutual funds. Mutual Funds typically redeem shares throughout the year, which result in a year end capital gains payout. ETF's, on the other hand, exchange stocks of the "same-kind" and incur much less overhead expense in comparison to mutual funds which reduce their overall need to sell/redeem shares in order to pay for their expenses. Rather than trading stocks individually, ETFs enable an investor to trade passively managed portfolios. Having a good balance of ETFs and Mutual Funds can prove to VASTLY diversify an individual portfolio.

### Money Market Funds

Money market funds are an extremely attractive product for investors interested in high liquidity with low growth, but substantially more than an average savings account. These funds are structured by investing in low risk, short term, debt instruments like Bank Certificates of Deposit, Commercial Papers, US Treasury Bonds, etc. Although they are extremely low risk, they do carry no guarantee of principal since they are, in fact, an investment product. This would be ideal for an investor who is saving money for a specified period of time and wants more growth than what's offered in a traditional savings account and has a very low risk, low reward approach to investing money, specifically short term.

### Options

In comparison to the variety of investment products covered so far, options are without a doubt the most unique, highest profit generating, and the most risky. Options are considered derivative products, meaning that the investor is not investing into stock of a company, but rather investing into a product that is based on the stock performance itself. Options are broken into two different, well, options. Calls or Puts. Before we get into these complex concepts it is imperative to understand a few key concepts.

First, and most importantly, options are contracts to purchase 100 shares of a stock at a set price, not a stock itself. Options are composed of a few elements (Maturity, Strike Price, Company, Type, & Premium). For example, a January 600 APPL Call at 50. Let's break this down piece by piece. First, (January) this represents the expiration month of an option contract. Option contracts typically expire on the third Friday of the expiration month at 4pm. Second, (600) this represents the strike price, which enables the investor to either purchase or sell the stock at that price. Third, (APPL) this is the ticker for the underlying stock, in this case, Apple. Fourth (Call) this is the type of option contract, either call or put. Lastly, (50) this is the premium for the contract. With options, it is essential to remember that these contracts represent the right to buy or sell 100 shares of the underlying stock. So, that premium represents the price per share to acquire the contract, which in this case (50*100) = $5000 premium.

A flexible aspect of options is that investor has the ability to buy or sell these contracts. When an investor buys an option, they are purchasing the right to either buy(call) or sell(put) shares at expiration at the strike price. Buying options gives the investor the RIGHT to exercise the option, without obligation, meaning the options can expire worthless. When an investor sells (shorts) an option, they are selling the right to either buy(call) or sell(put) shares at expiration at the strike price. Shorting options puts an obligation on the investor that they must fulfill the contract if exercised, regardless of the amount of profit or loss (hence why selling uncovered options is one of the riskiest forms of investing). Another critical element of options is understanding the bull and bear approach to selecting an option. In Finance, rather than there being the Birds and Bees, there's the Bears and Bulls. As scary as that sounds, these conflicting market perspectives are very simple to understand. Bulls (Bullish) investors believe that the market will continue to rise, that stocks and the economy are performing well and typically are characterized by a consistently optimistic perspective of potential market performance. On the other hand, Bears, have very poor opinions about the market. These are typically your very speculative investors that believe that markets are bound to drop and that stock will underperform expectations.

Lastly, one must understand is OTM, ITM, or ATM. ATM stands for "at the money." This means that at that time the option's underlying stock price is identical to the strike price of the option. ITM stands for "in the money." This means that at that time the option's underlying stock price is higher than the strike price of the option. OTM stands for "out of the money." This means that the option's underlying stock price is lower than the strike price of the option.

## Calls

Calls represent a derivative approach to taking advantage of increases in potential stock performance (Bullish). A call enables an investor to purchase a contract for the right to buy 100 shares of a stock at a set price in the future. The price that the investor pays for this option contract is called the premium. The price that the contract allows the investor to pay for the stock in the future is called the strike price. The date the investor is able to buy the stock at the strike price is called the maturity date. In these contracts, the investor is able to generate profit by purchasing the stock in the future at a lower strike price than what the stock is trading for.

For example, if ypu buy an Apple (AAPL) call option for a $1000 premium, with a strike price of $500 set to expire in October, and at expiration AAPL is trading at $600 then you would net a $9000 profit.

(($600 (market price) -$500 (strike price) )*100 = $10,000 - $1000 (premium paid)

Even though that sounds too easy and good to be true, the alternative risk is that if at expiration AAPL was trading at $520 rather than $600 you would net a loss of eight thousand dollars (($600-$520)*100) = $8000.

One of the great benefits of Calls, though, is that there is no obligation to exercise these options at the expiration date. That means that prior to expiration, if one could tell that the market price of the stock at expiration would not be greater than the strike price, they could cancel the option and just lose the premium paid, rather than experience the catastrophic loss potential. Clearly these products are extremely risky, but at the same time, if utilized strategically and analytically can be extremely profitable.

### Puts

The difference between a Put and a Call is simple: the CALL gives the contract owner the right to buy an underlying stock at a strike price with the interpretation that the stock price is going up (Bull approach), PUTS give the contract owner the right to sell an underlying stock at a strike price with the interpretation that the stock price is going to go down (Bear approach). So naturally, if investors profit from Calls if the stock price goes higher than the strike price, put investors profit if the market price drops lower than the strike price. Inversely to a call option, the put option generates profit because, at expiration, the option holder has the right to sell the put at a set price. If the stock price at expiration is lower than the strike price, the investor is able to profit from the difference between the two (minus the premium paid). Since the put gives the option holder the right to sell, the option holder at expiration will have to buy 100 shares of the underlying stock at the stock price and subsequently sell the stock at the strike price, hence why a lower stock price is essential to net profit.

For example, if you buy an Apple (AAPL) put option for a $1000 premium, with a strike price of $500, set to expire in October of 2021, and at expiration AAPL is trading at $400 then you would net a $9000 profit.

(($500 (strike price) -$400 (stock price) )*100 = $10,000 -
$1000 (premium paid)
That sounds like a great way to take advantage of a down market,
but the alternative risk is that if at expiration AAPL was trading
at $600 rather than $500 you would net a huge loss.
(($600-$500)*100) = $10,000

## Futures

Similar to the way that options investors are able to buy
and sell options contracts for the right/obligation to purchase
and sell stocks at a set date and time, a futures contract is a
derivative product that contractually obligates the transaction
of an asset at a set price, at expiration, regardless of the market
price. Considering the transactional nature of futures, these assets include real assets, such as commodities (crops, oil, metals)
but also include a wider variety of assets, such as stock market
indexes (S&P, Currency, Treasury bonds) making futures an attractive option to hedge an underlying investment.

One of the immediate differences between options and futures is the element of obligation. An options contract gives the
holder the option to exercise, or not, which alleviates the obligation of the investment based on the price of the underlying asset.
A futures contract obligates the buyer and seller to exchange the
underlying asset at the set price at expiration, regardless of its
price. At expiration, these assets can be physically delivered or
settled for cash, meaning that based on the exchange through
which they were purchased, some futures contracts may require
the underlying assets (ie. corn, wheat, oil) be physically delivered
to the buyer at expiration, as to where others may just settle the
contract with cash. Another unique characteristic of Futures is,
since they are trading multiple types of commodities, there are
different contract units based on the commodity in the contract.
For example, oil trades in units of 1,000 barrels, but corn trades
in units of 5000 bushels. This understanding is very important
when calculating the cost per unit for a futures contract.

From a business perspective, futures trading provides considerable profit opportunities for businesses to acquire commodities that they use for production at a discounted price, while also giving cash focused investors opportunities to generate a profit. For example, if an investor bought a futures contract on Corn at a $ 50, and at expiration Corn was trading at $ 50.65, they would have a .65 per bushel profit (remember, there are 5000 bushels in 1 unit). In order to capitalize on this profit potential, the investor would have to offset the buy side of the contract by selling it at the commodity's current market value before expiration, effectively closing the position and netting the investor the difference in cash, rather than delivery of the commodity. On the other hand, the investor is still subject to risk if the commodity's price were to drop, because they would have to sell the commodity at a loss to offset the contract.

While futures contracts can be utilized to leverage positive price fluctuations, they can also be utilized to speculate on negative price movements, as well. For example, if an investor speculates negative price movement, they are able to open a short selling position on a futures contract. This means that in order to profit from this position, they will purchase a futures contract on a commodity at the same expiration date and unit size, but at the market price of the underlying commodity. In order to net a positive profit, they would want the market price of the commodity to fall below the price of the original future contract to net a positive difference. On the other hand, if the underlying stock price rose above the price of the future contract price, this would result in a loss to the investor, very similar to the way that put options generate profit.

## Forwards

To this point we have become fairly comfortable with the concepts of Futures, defining it basically as a set legal agreement to buy or sell a commodity for a specific price at expiration. What differentiates a Forward contract from a future is that this contract is actually customizable. Unlike a Futures contract that is considered standardized, in a Forwards contract the commodity, the expiration, and the price can all be customized. Although both the Forwards and the Futures contracts can be settled for either cash or product, the Forwards contract can only be settled at the end of the contract, unlike the futures contract whose profits and losses can be settled daily. Another notable difference between the two contracts is that Futures are tradable on an exchange, as to where Forwards only trade OTC (Over the Counter).

Let's get into an example: say a major grain producer in the Southeast speculates a decline in the price of grain in the next 3 months when they plan to harvest their crop. So, to hedge the possibility of the price of Grain declining before the harvest, they enter into a futures contract with a financial institution where they contractually agree to exchange exactly 1000 bushels of Grain at $3.50 per bushel on a cash basis. Come the 3-month expiration, there are only a few possible options. If the market price for Grain is $3.50, both parties will settle the contract with no profit or loss to anyone. If the Market Price of Grain is above $3.50, then the producer will lose the difference between the contract price and the current market price per bushel. Lastly, if the market price is below the contract price, the producer will net the difference between the two as profit.

Clearly, while this product can be a very effective hedging strategy for large corporations to hedge commodities and currencies against changes in interest rates and exchange rates, it also carries a clear degree of risk. Since these contracts are customizable and only exchange at expiration, this creates a substantial risk for financial institutions because they have no way to negate or mitigate the risk from price fluctuations that occur prior to expiration, which leaves them at a much greater risk for default risk on the agreement because they have no protection.

# INVESTING IN REAL ESTATE

*"Real estate cannot be lost or stolen, nor can it be carried away. Purchased with common sense, paid for in full, and managed with reasonable care, it is about the safest investment in the world. "* **— Franklin D. Roosevelt**


In today's society, the majority of wealthy entrepreneurs, investors, and business moguls invest in some form of real estate. Real estate offers investors the opportunity to invest in a tangible asset, whose value can be influenced directly by the investor. For example, if an investor purchased a single lot of undeveloped land for $50,000 and had the time and resources to invest $60,000 to develop a very nice modernized home, that investor would have invested $110,000 for the project, but if the average home in the area (similar in style and build) costs around $200,000. That investor nets a $90,000 profit potential. Coupling that with the concept of leverage, and the possibility that the investor could use other peoples' money to pay for the property, makes real estate investing an extremely attractive and adaptable investment.

There are a few key strategies that one can use to invest in real estate, and even more ways to make money from it, but in this context, we will cover: Flipping, Buy/Hold, Developing a Rental Portfolio, and REITS.


### Flipping Real Estate

Flipping real estate has become a very transparent and popular form of investing. We see numerous shows about it on television, podcasts, youtubers showing their projects, and even large-scale companies that teach investors how to do it. So, to put it plainly, there is an endless supply of resources to learn more about the strategy and specifics. In general, flipping real estate is the process of investing in a property that is undervalued (more than likely due to some degree of physical damage, outdating, etc.) and putting in the capital and resources to turn it into a modern-day property for a reasonable profit. From there it is simply rinse, wash, and repeat. A number of investors make a living flipping multiple projects per year, and strategically using certain renovated properties as rentals. Given the dynamics of this strategy, it is clear that the keys to profit are either low acquisition costs or low renovation, and in a perfect world, both.

Some things that you can do as a novice investor are: attending real estate networking events in your area, networking with other flippers, making connections with wholesalers, and contractors, and doing as much research as you can online. This will develop a network of teachers, suppliers, and laborers to work on the renovation. Wholesalers are staple suppliers in this industry because they offer premarket properties (properties you can't find online) at prices well below market value. They only catch is that they typically are all cash transactions, which just require more planning and capital up front, but leaves an investor debt free after the project. Taking the time to build solid relationships with contractors, or understanding the costs of renovation, are critical to finding the ideal flip. Another aspect that is equally important is understanding how to research comps (prices of comparable properties in your area) to estimate end value. There are a number of resources/apps to help you do this, but one effective entry level exercise is to compare prices on Zillow to get an idea and develop your own preference on resources to help you along the way.

## Buy/Hold

The Buy/Hold strategy is a classic strategy to passively take advantage of appreciating property values on real estate. As the name suggests, an investor would purchase a property with the intention of selling the property after a certain number of years to sell at a higher price based on the appreciation in the area. This could involve living in the property, renovating the property over time, renting out the property and netting the income, or just buying it, leaving it and selling it. There are many different ways to make this strategy work in the meantime.

### Developing a Rental Portfolio

Many real estate moguls we see today, like Grant Cardone or Carl Berg, create these massive scales of money from developing a portfolio of rental properties. This concept basically follows the same rinse, wash, repeat cycle of identifying a property, acquiring the property, renovating, and renting (buy/hold). Developing a portfolio of properties could consist of however many properties you want, with all different styles and market orientations.

One of the key real estate terms to remember when it comes to property selection is **Cap Rate.** This number basically represents annual Return on investment, and is calculated by dividing the Net Operating Income by the Purchase Price. So, an investment with an 8% cap rate will return 8% of the purchase price per year in income: meaning mathematically if you were to finance this project, the difference between your interest rate and the cap rate would equal your net profit, so long as a tenant(s) occupied the property. Some key things to consider when selecting a rental property to invest in are: location, comps, acquisition (cash/finance - both), cap rate, and tenant occupation.

### REITS

REIT stands for Real Estate Investment Trust; this trust operates as a company by pooling together assets from investors and utilizing those assets to acquire income generating real estate. The trust will do all the hands-on work of maintenance and daily operations, while the investors receive dividends (their shared interest) in the profit from the real estate. These REITS are traded on the stock market, making them far more liquid than actual real estate, but offers the same aspect of passive income. Each REIT invests in different particular projects or sectors, but most are composed of multi-family properties and commercial real estate. These basically give an investor the opportunity to invest in income generating real estate without having to do the leg work to acquire it or maintain it.

## Notes

In real estate, notes function very similarly to the banking notes we covered earlier in the book. In a conventional real estate transaction, a buyer provides a down payment to obtain a loan and signs a note (mortgage) promising to pay the mortgage company a certain amount (principal+interest) to satisfy the agreement. With a real estate note, a buyer doesn't obtain a loan (which situates the mortgage company to pay the seller the principal amount, and the mortgagee then theoretically owns the property, and charges the buyer interest), they instead pay the seller a monthly price plus interest until the transaction is satisfied. Essentially, the seller becomes the lender.

These notes then become very attractive investment opportunities because these notes can actually be sold to investors individually, or as a package. An extremely attractive aspect of the note is that if the buyer (the one making payments) defaults on the note terms, the owner of the note will then hold ownership of the property. This is a unique investment, with a proportional risk. For example, let's say you purchase a note for $70,000 with $600 monthly payments for 5 years on a house that has a market value of approximately $135,000. The investor will immediately start receiving those $600 monthly payments for 5 years. If the buyer fails to make payments, the investor can foreclose on the property (which obviously incurs its own fees) but that buyer will then own a $135,000 market value home for roughly $70,000, plus foreclosure fees (minus payments received), which they can then turn around and sell for roughly $50,000 in profit, or initiate their own rent on the property and continue to receive payments that they can later sell.

Clearly, notes are a very flexible and attractive investment product, but should be approached with caution as each carries varying terms/conditions/costs etc. It would be beneficial to consult a real estate professional that specializes in these transactions.

## What about Taxes?

As with any investment strategy, real estate investing also carries its share of tax burden. Similar to stock trading, long term and short term capital gains do apply to real estate transactions, but thankfully there is a way to avoid these potentially substantial tax situations. **1031 Exchange** is the legal "exchange" of real estate investment properties that defer the capital gain tax. To show how these work, let's look at an example. If you bought a house and flipped it in 6 months, the sale of the house would result in a short term capital gains tax on the profit from that sale, but with the 1031 exchange this gives you 45 days to identify one or more properties to invest that growth in, and 180 days to close on one of those properties. This exchange defers the short term capital gain to now a long term capital gain (assuming you keep the property for at least 6 months to make it a year since the first transaction).

Although the real estate investor does not tangibly realize this profit up front, the exchange can be a great way to avoid the short term capital gains and only have to pay long term gains on the money at a later date, for a savvy buy/hold investor looking to build rental income on properties, this could be a very attractive strategy to avoid taxes all together, at least in the immediate future.

# RETIREMENT VEHICLES

*"If you fail to plan, you are planning to fail"* — **Benjamin Franklin**

Planning for retirement is a concept that practically every professional has faced at some point in their career, but what does this actually mean? Most professionals'[ understanding of retirement is limited to knowing that they are contributing a certain percentage of their income into their companies' pre-structured 401K or IRA, with little to no understanding of what that product is investing in, the tax advantages or disadvantages of these products, or whether what they are contributing is enough to sustain them in retirement. In complete reality, most people are unaware of what they need in retirement to sustain their cost of living, or achieve their long term goals. So rather than start this chapter with developing your knowledge of retirement strategies, we'll start this chapter with YOU. Because, at the end of the day, when it comes to winning at finance, planning for retirement, or just getting better in general, it is up to you to decide what you're going to do and how hard you're going to work to achieve it. Working with a professional in the finance industry can go a long way in terms of calculating the adjusted cost of living in the year you plan to retire, helping you develop a strategy that works for you in terms of how to allocate your money and how that affects your retirement savings, as well as helping you select products that are advantageous in terms of taxes, growth, and long term funding.

Before we move on to learning about the various vehicles that one can use to plan for retirement, we would highly encourage you as our reader to take the time to consider your goals for the future and research your current retirement vehicles that you are using. Now that that is out of the way, let's get to it!

## IRA

In the world of retirement planning, the IRA is the staple product. IRA stands for Individual Retirement Account, and is an account specifically designed to offer tax incentives, low expenses, and a risk averse vehicle to save for retirement. These IRA's can utilize the majority of the investment vehicles we have covered thus far (stocks, bonds, mutual funds, ETF's, etc.) to offer limited risk on growing the account. Although very simple, these accounts come in a variety of options that are structured differently, and have a number of limitations.

Let's start with general rules and limitations: IRA's generally come with set rules and limitations. First is income. One of the first rules to understand about IRA's is that they utilize an investor's pre-tax dollars, and that an investor can only fund these accounts with taxable income (you can't use child support, social security, or income from investments). This rule is in place because, depending on the type of IRA you choose to use, you will be able to deduct those contributions from your taxable income (up to a certain amount). So, for example, if you made $50,000 last year and contributed $4000 to your company sponsored IRA, you would only report $44,000 in income on your taxes. Although this up-front incentive is very attractive to professionals as they progress through their professional careers and navigate tax brackets, it does come at a cost on the back end. Once investors begin receiving distributions from the IRA, they will have to pay taxes based on their current income tax bracket.

Another important element of IRA's to understand are the contribution limitations. IRA accounts limit the amount of taxable income an investor is able to invest into their IRA account. For those under the age of 50, this amount is limited to $6000 per year, and if you're over 50 a catchup provision is allowed that will grant you to invest an extra $1000 per year, totaling $7000. If an individual were to get an early start at retirement savings, this limitation would not impede their ability to reach a certain goal, but, on the other hand, if a person were to wait too late in their career, it would virtually impossible with just an IRA account.

The last, and in our opinion, the most important limitations of an IRA account are the early withdrawal fees and RMDs. IRA's are structured to be able to make distributions to an investor beginning at age 59. This means that if an investor were to try to take distributions, or withdraw funds from their IRA before age 59 ½, they would be subject to a 10% early withdrawal penalty, in addition to the full income taxation, as well. This does not mean that an investor can only contribute to the IRA until age 59 ½. They actually have until age 72 to contribute to the account, but they cannot take money from it until age 59 ½. Now, there are some exceptions when it comes to early withdrawal penalties from your IRA (these are listed in the chart below). RMDs stand for required minimum distributions. This means that after the age of 59 ½ an investor has until the age of 72 to start taking distributions from the account (meaning you can't just let the account sit and grow until passed the age of 72). Failure to take distributions by the age of 72 will result in a tax penalty of 50% on the required distribution amount.

As an employee/professional that is given options to invest through their company's structured plan, it is very important to request information on these accounts and make sure their structure, goals, and investments align with your goals for the future. If an employee cannot meet their retirement goals through their employer's structured IRA, they can also structure their own IRA called a SDIRA (Self Directed IRA). This gives more control and decision making for the IRA, and also does not restrict investment decisions to just stocks, bonds, and mutual funds. In order to establish an SDIRA, one should consult an advisor, or check online through most online brokerage services (Fidelity, Merrill Edge, etc.). Obviously, although a key staple, this IRA account comes with its fair share of limitations, including the risk and longevity of the account.

Although IRAs are structured to take low risk/conservative

positions, they still are exposed to market risk, since they are connected to the stock market. The income from these accounts are not guaranteed for life. Although one may save their entire professional career, unless they take the time with a professional to calculate their projected cost of living and the subsequent amount the account would need, they do put themselves at a greater risk of running out of money.

### Roth IRA

The kin to the infamous IRA account is the also well recognized: Roth IRA. The immediate difference between a Roth and a traditional IRA is that the IRA uses pre-tax dollars (meaning the distributions are taxed) and the Roth uses post-tax dollars, meaning the distributions are tax free. These accounts also do not have RMDs, meaning that an investor can contribute into them as long as they like without having to withdraw anything. They still require contributions from only earned income, just like the traditional IRA. They also have the same contribution limits (younger than 50, $6000. Older than 50, $7000). A notable point to consider about Roths is that their contributions are not tax deductible, since it utilizes post tax dollars. Clearly, Roths and IRAs share very similar characteristics, but cater to different tax preferences. The advantage of knowing these products is that an investor can contribute to both a Roth and traditional IRA, at the same time, so long as that overall annual investment does not exceed the contribution limit (Younger than 50, $6000. Older than 50, $7000). Although these products are similar, selecting which product to invest in can have very different outcomes in terms of income at retirement. Taking the time to consult with a professional can alleviate the stress or confusion in trying to appropriately utilize either of these options

### SEP/Simple IRA

SEP & Simple IRAs are both grouped together because they are oriented towards small business owners, self-employed professionals, independent contractors, etc. Although these retirement vehicles are structured for these professionals, it is also valuable to understand how they work if you are an employee, so that you can understand why an employer may choose this option. SEP stands for Self-employed pension. This structured retirement vehicle allows a business owner to establish one for their employees, in which the owner can structure contributions that are then deducted from the business owner's income. The limitation on this form of pension is that the employees can not contribute to the plan and, once employees start taking withdrawals from their pension, they are taxed as ordinary income. For employers, their contributions to the pension are limited to 25% of their overall compensation, or $57,0000, whichever is less.

Simple IRA, stands for, savings incentive match plan for employees, which is very similar to an SEP IRA, but allows the employees to make contributions, and subsequently requires the employer to make contributions, as well. All contributions are tax deductible for both the employee and employer, and limited to $13,500 per year, with a catch-up contribution of $3000 for investors age 50 and older.

## IRA Comparison

Listed below is a chart to help remember the limitations and boundaries of the various IRA accounts we just discussed. All charts listed are current as of September 18, 2020 but the contribution limits and taxation exclusions can change over time, so it is important to consult a professional accountant or tax expert to determine the accurate figures.

| IRA Type | Investor | Tax Deductible | Taxable Distributions | RMDs? |
|---|---|---|---|---|
| Traditional | Tax Paying Employee | Yes | Yes | Yes |
| Roth | Tax Paying Employee | No | No | No |
| SEP | Business Owners/ Self Employed | Yes (limited) | Yes | Yes |
| Simple | Business Owners/ Self Employed | Yes | Yes | Yes |

## Traditional 401K

The 401 K has become a very popular retirement vehicle, offered by larger companies to increase employee savings for retirement and retention. 401ks are tax advantaged automatically, withholding desired contribution amounts from an employee's paycheck. They use pretax dollars, which lowers an investor's taxable income, resulting in more upfront savings. Along with the employee's designated contributions, employers are also able to match these contributions up to 100%. Similar to a Traditional IRA, these 401ks also have taxed withdrawals. For investors under the age of 50, these accounts carry a combined (employer/employee) contribution limit of 100% of the employees income, or $57,000 (whichever is less), $19,500 of which is capped for the employee contribution. For investors over the age of 50, the combined (employer/employee) contribution limit is 100% of the employee's income or $63,500 (whichever is less), $26,000 is capped for the employee contribution (catch up provision of $6,500).

## Roth 401K

The Roth 401k carries an identical relationship to the Roth IRA. This account is parallel to the Traditional 401K, but utilizes post-tax income to fund the account, which means the contribution is not withheld pre-tax. These accounts do not offer the ability to lower taxable income like the Traditional 401K, but are structured to offer tax free withdrawals once they begin.

## 401K Penalties/Limitations

Similar to IRAs, 401Ks carry full taxation, and 10% early withdrawal penalties for investors trying to withdraw funds prior to age 59 ½. These accounts also carry the same RMD (required minimum distributions) standards as traditional IRAs, meaning at age 72 investors must start withdrawing a certain percentage of the account, or face full income taxation penalty on 50% of the required minimum distribution amount, unless that employee is still working for the business. 401ks also carry early withdrawal exceptions, but you should consult with a professional, or do adequate research, to identify the allowable exceptions that qualify for this year.

### Rolling Over Retirement Vehicles

Up to this point, we have seen that adequate employers typically offer a variety of retirement investment options for their employees. One thing that is common in modern business is that you, as a professional (young or experienced), have more than likely changed jobs with different companies. So what about those retirement plans? Where does that money go? What can you do with it?

With each of these employer sponsored retirement plans, they are held with a certain broker or retirement company. The first thing that should be done is to reach out to that employer to figure out what, or who, they use for the retirement plans, and then coordinate with that company to get information on the account. As the investor, you are more than welcome to keep the retirement with the company, if you so choose. We would highly recommend at least reaching out, though, to get information about the account so that you can make sure it aligns with your goals, and you know how it is performing.

If you choose not to leave that account with the broker, or your former employer, then rest assured that there are plenty of options available to you. You can choose to rollover that account to your current employer, if they also offer retirement plans. In most cases it is as simple as just reaching out to HR and getting directions on how to appropriately transfer the old account to your current company. You can choose to rollover that account to an investment brokerage. This option would be very attractive to an investor that left a previous company, or is planning on leaving their current company, knowing that their next job does not have retirement plan options. With this option you would consult an advisor/financial professional who can rollover that 401k, or old company, IRA into a rollover IRA. You would then work together in deciding the appropriate investments, goals, etc.

Naturally, with all things investing, taxes are always a consideration. Before choosing which investment product to rollover your previous account into, it is imperative to know whether that account, or the next account, is a Roth or Traditional. If you choose to rollover a 401K or IRA into a Roth IRA, you will owe full income taxes on that rolled over amount because the Roth is a post-tax product. This could result in massive taxation, based on your bracket. But, if you roll that traditional IRA or 401K into a Traditional IRA, the taxes will continue to defer because the products match. Rolling over a Roth 401K or IRA offers much more flexibility because taxes have already been paid on the money, but naturally if you choose to rollover over a Roth account into a Traditional, you will no longer receive that tax break once withdrawals begin.

This knowledge can serve as a valuable tool when developing your overall retirement plan, and should always play a pivotal role in deciding your long-term employment. As always, it is valuable to either do very extensive research, or simply consult with a professional when planning the utilization or conversion of these retirement plans. Remember, it's never too early to start saving for retirement, but it can definitely become too late. Taking the time early in your career to establish a base plan, and working continuously to achieve those goals, will net you greater peace of mind and body as you progress throughout your career.

# LIFE INSURANCE

*"Life insurance is like a parachute; if you don't have it the first time you need it. There is no chance"* — **Luis A. Ortiz Haddock**

Life insurance is one of the most secure and effective aspects of a long-term generational plan. If you have a family/close loved ones, investing in life insurance carries a number of substantial benefits; including: alleviating them from financial burden if something happens to you, establishing a tax advantaged estate to wrap other investments/real estate around to leave to your loved ones that will avoid the involvement of the courts, creating large amounts of generational wealth for your loved ones at a small fraction of the cost, providing additional financial support for yourself if you were to become disabled, and paying off debt ahead of time. With all these benefits, life insurance also comes in a variety of options and additional features (riders). Similar to planning for retirement, establishing a life insurance policy in the earlier stages of your life will be more cost effective than waiting for the later stages because of the increased liability as you get older. Also, establishing a life insurance policy earlier in your planning process offers you that level of protection for much longer.

When it comes to selecting the ideal life insurance policy for yourself there are a few different types of policies to choose from, each having distinct benefits and features that make them attractive. These life insurance policies can be whole, term, or universal. So how much life insurance do you need? This is a common question, and one that advisors/agents will all tell differently, based on what types of products they sell/ have access to. The fact of the matter really is: it depends. Based on stage of life, income, dependents, outstanding debts, life goals, current assets, value of investments, etc. There are so many other pieces that can come into play when determining how much life insurance someone needs. One method of thinking is: "How much do I need to have a large enough death benefit to cover any debts?" One may also consider wanting to leave money behind for loved ones-helping to pay for college, or leaving something to help on a first home.

The payment for these policies is called premium. The premiums on these life insurance policies are calculated based on the insured's age, height, weight, job, and habits. If you have a more hazardous job, or unhealthy habits/ lifestyle, you can expect the premiums to be higher than that of someone with an overall healthier profile. Let's take a look at each of these options to see what they offer and how they could fit into your future financial plan.

### Whole Life Insurance

Whole life insurance is a permanent life insurance policy that offers protection for the life of the insured with a set death benefit, and payment for these policies are the same throughout the duration. An added benefit of a whole life insurance policy is that the cash value of the account accumulates throughout its duration, while gaining interest. An investor is able to accumulate a growing source of equity within the policy which they can actually access throughout the duration of the policy, through either withdrawals or a loan. Investors can contribute to the growth of this equity by "overpaying" on the premium of the policy. An added tax advantage of this access to capital is that the withdrawals/loans are tax free up to the amount of premium paid. If these withdrawals/loans are not returned, or paid back into the policy, they are taken against the death benefit, meaning that the policy owner has access to the money they invested.

One of the great pieces about life insurance is the ability

to over fund it. This process of overfunding is done by paying in more than the minimum premiums for the policy. By over funding a whole life policy, it will build up what is called "cash value." The insurance company will give you a return/ dividend on this money in cash value, allowing it to operate like a low risk investment portfolio. The returns on the cash value will differ based on the company, what type of product, etc., but there will always be something. Many of these accounts will come out to a guaranteed four percent per year!

### Term Life Insurance

To put it simply, if whole life covers the entire life of the insured, term insurance policies are designed to cover a designated amount of time for the insured (for example, a 10-year term policy is in place for ten years). This policy offers protection for the insured within its designated duration, as well as massive savings in regards to premium dollars paid in. Generally, it is a good idea to lean towards term insurance, due to the cost difference. It can be a third of the cost, can be used for when you most need it, and can oftentimes have much more lenient requirements to obtain it. But there are some things that term insurance can't do. The downfall of this policy is that it does not offer cash value accumulation like that of a whole life insurance policy. The premiums on these policies are fixed (level) throughout the term (years) of the policy, but these premiums are expected to adjust based on the term of the policy. Typically, the longer the term, the higher the premium. At the end of these terms, policy owners can either extend/renew their policy or let it expire and get a new policy.

### Universal Life Insurance

Universal Life Insurance, sometimes referred to as variable Life Insurance, is very different from other types of life insurance. Generally, one of the variables in these policies will fluctuate: be it the death benefit, or premium dollars paid in. Because of having an option to fluctuate with the death benefit, or varying premium requirements, the life insurance company is often able to de-risk some of their portfolio's liability, ultimately working its way down into savings that are enjoyed by the policyholders/owners.

Universal Life Insurance policies are a type of permanent policy, allowing owners to lock in coverage for as long as they can pay premiums. Also, similar to whole life policies, universal life policies allow for accumulation of cash value inside of the policy. The accumulation may be a guaranteed percentage, or may be based on an index/ option into the market. Options were discussed in an earlier section in this book, and they are a common investment vehicle for insurance companies to grow their cash reserves. By using an option, insurance companies are able to enjoy the large possible upswing in the market, while taking only a minimal loss in the event of market downturns. By using this method, insurance companies are oftentimes able to deliver larger returns, all while eliminating downside risk. In these types of policies, investors can expect to make between 0 and 10.5% (actual returns will vary by company. These are just examples). There's a guaranteed floor, meaning that money invested into these types of policies will never go down, or lose money. For this reason, many of these accounts are becoming more and more popular with people today.

### Life Insurance Riders

Life insurance is clearly a simple, yet effective, and extremely valuable resource to add to anyone's holistic plan. Within life insurance policies, agents/advisors are able to utilize additional features to tailor a policy to you or your family's needs. These additional features are called Riders.

The first of these that we'll take a look at is the Accelerated **Death Benefit Rider**, also known as living benefits. This policy addition allows for the owner to tap into the death benefit of the policy in the event that something catastrophic happens. The causes vary by carrier, but generally if the insured is not able to carry out two of six daily activities (ex: washing self, transferring to the bathroom, feeding self, etc.) then the money is eligible to be used. With living benefits, the owner is able to tap into a large portion (up to ninety or ninety-five percent) of the death benefit. These funds can be used on whatever: medical bills, mortgage payments, childcare, etc.

Another common rider with insurance policies is a **Return of Premium Rider**. This allows for the policy holder to receive back all of their paid premium payments in the event that they don't use the policy during their allotted term.

As we all know, when it comes to death, oftentimes it is unexpected and more so often, accidents happen. The **Accidental Death Rider** provides an additional payment amount to the death benefit in the events that the insured were to die from some sort of accident. Typically with this rider, the beneficiary of the insured is paid both the face amount of the policy (all the money invested in the policy - the additional payment) and the death benefit. Although clearly a reasonable rider, take time to consult the agent/advisor issuing the policy because different companies have different definitions for the term "accident".

For those reading this that are the independent source of income for their families, or plan to leave their insurance policy benefits to those that will will be younger in age and would rather disperse the benefit in payments, rather than a lump sum could utilize the **Family Income Benefit Rider**. That takes the death benefit of the insured and breaks it into even, steady payments through a set number of years, determined by the insured.

When it comes to planning for the future, one of the most emotionally and financially difficult decisions to make is when it comes to providing Long-Term Care for a loved one. For those looking to alleviate the financial worry involved in this process, they can situate a life insurance policy on a loved one with, and include a **Long-Term Care Rider**. This rider provides monthly payments in the event the insured has to stay at a nursing home, or receive home health care. This sort of strategic planning can be a huge difference maker when it comes to affording the quality of life that both you and your loved ones deserve.

Knowing one's goals helps in securing life insurance. Many people use these products as a safety umbrella for their family, and some use them as a super powered investment vehicle. As previously mentioned, some types of life insurance policies have guaranteed interest accumulation, some have a guaranteed zero downside risk, and some can be used creatively to pay off debts and expenses by utilizing a range of riders and policy types. For someone looking to invest their money, life insurance is a great component to creating a well-rounded financial plan.

# DEVELOPING A PLAN

*"It's not how much money you make, but how much money you keep, how hard it works for you, and how many generations you keep it for "* — **Robert Kiyosaki**

Let's say that you work hard and earn some money. You decide to begin setting back some of your money to invest, so you find a great investment vehicle (pick any that you like) and you put one hundred dollars into it. This is a really great investment opportunity, and you'll be earning ten percent per year! So, you invest your money, and at the end of the first year you have your original one hundred dollars, plus the ten percent interest that you earned, so one hundred and ten dollars. Awesome. After the first year, you are happy, and decide that you plan to reinvest your profits, leaving all of the money there for the next year. At the end of the second year, you wind up with another ten percent in interest. The kicker here is that you earned that on your original investment, also known as the principal, and the interest you earned in year one!

Ten percent interest on one hundred dollars is ten dollars, and then ten percent on ten dollars (money earned from year one) is another dollar. The original one hundred dollars is now one hundred and twenty-one dollars. The third year you will end up earning twelve dollars and ten cents, the fourth year you earn thirteen dollars and thirty-one cents, and so on. As you can see, the longer you have your money invested, the more you make. You begin to earn interest on interest that you have just earned. Then you begin to earn interest on that money! Compound interest gets pretty crazy, but this concept is why starting early, investing your money, and developing a plan is the KEY to Winning at Finance. There is a lot of money to be made. All it takes is a plan, time and commitment.

### How Do I Create a Plan?

Throughout the course of this book we have covered a wide variety of financial products, ranging from stocks, to real estate, to life insurance. Although all of these products are very effective to reach a set monetary goal, without a plan in place, one will fail to realize the full financial power that lies with utilizing all of these products together. The first, and most critical concept, about developing this plan is to understand that there is no right answer. An individual's financial plan should be tailored to fit their individual income, goals, and responsibilities. With that in mind, we will break down a few general principles/tactics that one can utilize to develop their own individual plan.

### Set Goals

Finances and money are no different than personal health or your profession, without clear cut goals (short, medium, and long term) one cannot hope to fully maximize their finances or achieve their desired income goals. The goal setting process can be as simple, or as intricate, as you would like, but a great rule of thumb is to follow the **S.M.A.R.T Goals** concept. S.M.A.R.T stands for Specific, Measurable, Achievable, Relevant, & Time bound. Determine any financial goals that you have: decide on what age you want to retire, how much money you need to spend each year in retirement, how long you think you may live (based on your health, family history, national averages, etc.), and what you hope to leave behind for your family. Start with the end in mind, and then work backwards.

### Analyze your Finances

Financial analysis is far more than just a job title or approach to making a business more money. On a personal level, financial analysis is one of the single most important steps in creating a long-term plan. In 2020 there are so many resources to use that will help you with this process, from Tiller Money (which connects your bank account information and breaks out analysis into categorized google sheets to share with your family and check on the go) to Mint (an app on your phone that integrates with your bank accounts to offer weekly analysis and categorized spending breakdown). We recommend using an app, or online program, in order to get an idea of how much money you are bringing in, how much money you are spending, and areas that you can improve. This will let you look at what types of purchases you are making often, and will give you a baseline of where you are.

### Create a Budget

After getting to know yourself from a financial perspective, finding out how you spend money and what you spend it on, it is pivotal to take the time to learn your finances. What this means is sit down and go through all your subscriptions, your services, your spending habits, etc. and cut out the things that you genuinely have no need or interest in. Typically, whenever people go through this exercise, we find that they will find at least three things that they did not know they were paying for or have no interest in paying for it anymore.

After taking the time to lean out your finances, now we have to figure out how and what we're going to spend our money on. We have found that one of the most effective ways to accomplish this is by breaking your spending into categorized percentages. You can configure your own categories, but we have found that breaking your income down to Essentials (Bills, Gas, Groceries, etc.), Wants (clothes, fine dining, weekend trips), and Savings (Retirement, Savings Account, Investing) have proven to be an effective base to configure your plan.

### 50/30/20

Now that we have a base layout of what we spend our

money on, we have to understand how we are going to spend our money. Once again, these percentages can be adjusted or flip flopped to what you feel comfortable with, but a great base to start with is 50% Essentials, 30% Wants, 20% Savings. Taking the time to break down your finances to this basic percentage-based method, will allow you to fit within a budget that expands as you make more money. For people that may be motivated by what they can have or buy, this would serve a great benchmark to work harder to earn more, so you can subsequently have more and invest more (which means you'll make more money), rather than just having more and investing less. We have seen that younger investors have more freedom to sit in the 50/30/20 split in comparison to older professionals, who may have to allocate 30%+ to savings in order to afford retirement, so here is another example of how starting early saves more and allows you to make and have more.

### How Should I Spend my 20%?

Here lies the million-dollar question, the key to creating wealth and becoming rich, and the correct answer is: it's up to you. Quite frankly there are hundreds of ways to create substantial wealth through investing, many of which are far beyond the scope of this book. The best part is that you don't need any high dollar strategy, or hundreds of thousands of dollars to create financial freedom and wealth from investing. All you need is a plan and commitment. If you save and commit to a plan that you, or a professional, have developed for yourself, you can greatly increase your chances of achieving, if not exceeding, both personal and monetary goals. In the hands of the right person, the products and knowledge detailed throughout this book could be the piece of information that an investor needs in order to develop a plan to reach their goals. So although it's not in your best interest for us to tell you exactly what to do, since we don't know your situation, let's walk through a couple of concepts to consider when determining how to invest your 20%!

## Get an Idea of How Much Money You Need

One of the largest issues when it comes to retirement and planning for the future is understanding how much money you need to save in the first place. Consulting a professional can serve you a world of good in terms of predicting inflation rates/cost of living, getting an idea of costs associated with your ideal lifestyle as well as retirement, and getting a base prediction as to how much money you need total, how much money you need per month, and how much money you need to leave in order to alleviate both you and your family's family burden.

## Paying off Debt

As we discussed in the earlier portions of this book, the banks make a fortune from the interest they charge for loans issued to customers which include mortgages, car loans, credit cards, etc. From a consumer standpoint that means that in our lifetime we spend thousands if not hundreds of thousands in extra interest payments. So an effective point that one should consider when investing is investing in products or utilizing strategies where one could allocate their growth towards paying off debt. Some product options that could be utilized to do this would include, life insurance, stock and mutual fund dividends, real estate.

Another strategic approach to paying off debt is capitalizing on refinancing and debt consolidation opportunities. Taking advantage of lower interest rates through refinancing can save thousands of dollars in interest, for example if you have a 30 year fixed mortgage for $200,000 at a 4.5% interest rate, your total loan amount will be $364,813 (200,000 principal/ $164,813 interest) with payments of $1,013 per month. Say 5 years pass and you've got a $160,000 balance left on your loan, interest rates drop, your credit goes, and you look to refinance, if you could refinance for a 25 year fixed mortgage at a 3.6% interest rate, you would now only pay $809 per month ( $204 savings per month, $2,448 per year) and would now only have a loan amount of $242,881 and a savings of roughly $81,932 in interest.

### Reinvesting in Real Estate

Real estate investing carries a number of options, costs, and rewards. Before choosing a project or investment strategy, one should take the time to solidify that the capital needed only takes up a certain percentage of their savings (lower than 40%) and that your monthly income is enough to sustain the investment given any property damages or tenant vacancies. Allocating saved profits towards real estate is a great way to diversify your asset portfolio while also generating passive income that can then be reinvested into more streams of passive income. In our opinion, flipping houses carry a clear element of risk given the amount of capital needed to invest to hopefully secure a certain profit margin. But investing into a property to rent can net very positive long-term results whether it be residential or commercial. Many real estate investors create their fortunes by cyclically investing and reinvesting into more properties for streams of passive income and equity.

### Diversify Your Assets

In Real estate the key term is location, location, location. In the world of investing it is diversification, diversification, diversification. Diversifying your assets reduces the overall risk of your portfolio and increases your potential for continuous growth of your portfolio. This is possible because most of the investment classes operate with the ability to invest in different sectors, investing in different sectors across different asset closet gives you a balancing growth chart where losses in one sector/asset can be negated or overcome by gains in another sector/asset. One could achieve this diversification by simultaneously investing in 401k, Options, bonds, real estate, mutual funds,etc. Diversification is an extremely important aspect of Winning at finances, and although you may not have enough capital to invest in multiple products simultaneously, it would be valuable to utilize this guide to step back and evaluate what you products you may already be using, or are available to you, and then strategically develop your portfolio from there. When considering this diversification, it is imperative to consult with a professional when developing the structure or doing very extensive research.

### "Mortgage Protection"

With that being said, there are some places to start that are "best practices." First, many advisors will start by looking at your debt. A new term for life insurance arose a few years ago: "mortgage protection insurance." Advisors began to discover the people hated buying life insurance. They did not like the name, and related it too strongly to their death. Because of that, agents around the country began to rename the same type of policies "mortgage protection insurance." These policies are essentially a life insurance policy with a death benefit large enough to cover the owner's debts (mostly their mortgage). Some of these policies are sold as universal life policies, where the death benefit will decrease as time goes on, and as the owner pays off more of the mortgage.

### Infinite Banking

For investors who find a need to establish a system to pay off debt, while also establishing a lifelong insurance policy, they might consider establishing their own "infinite banking system". As was the case with mortgage protection insurance, life insurance agents have had to get creative with the naming of their products/ services over the years in an effort to sell more life insurance, without having the conversation about insurance. One of these methods is the infinite banking system. This is a process that has existed for many years, and has been used by some famous people and large corporations. For example, Ray Kroc used policy loans from his life insurance to help finance McDonalds.

Walt Disney used his policy to help pay for Disneyland. JC Penney used his life insurance policy to keep the retail giant afloat during some very tough times.

Whole life insurance policies accrue cash value, that then earns interest inside of the policies. Interest rates on these vary depending on the provider/policy. The idea behind infinite banking is that an investor will begin saving money in their policy, letting it grow, and then will begin taking loans against their money. Notice the distinction: against, rather than from. By using the money inside of the policy as collateral for a loan, the original money is allowed to continue growing and earning interest. Most times, the policy loan has an interest rate lower than the interest rate being earned on the cash value, so the owner will be able to save on interest payments on the loan, all while continuing to make money.

It is important to consider that these policies allocate a percentage of cash value into paying for the insurance policy over a certain number of years. So as an investor allocates money to the policy, they only have a certain percentage of cash value available to them, once the insurance portion of the policy is paid for, the insured will then be able to effectively grow their cash value based on the interest stipulated in the policy, which is typically 4%-6%.

So what are some applications of this concept? Well, because the policy owner can use these loans for anything they deem fit, they can: Access cash to help with emergencies (J.C. Penney did this to weather a financial struggle), buy a business (Ray Kroc used his policy to help buy McDonalds), open a new business (Walt Disney used his policy to help fund Disneyland), and pay off your debts, including your mortgage (this is the system that our team uses every day to help families get out of debt in a much faster amount of time, while still allowing them to save for retirement)

For years, many people have taken advantage of this opportunity. They have invested money into these policies, taken a policy loan to pay off a debt (generally the owner's smallest debt, or one with the highest interest rate). Upon payment of that debt, investors reallocate all previous payments back into the policy in order to pay off the loan and grow cash value faster. Then, when available money is large enough, another policy loan is taken against the cash value, allowing the owner to pay off the next debt. This process is repeated until all debts are paid off. This process has been called many different names, but the overall idea is the same. Many times, this system can be used to help someone pay off a thirty-year mortgage in a third or half of the time. This strategy is not to replace retirement planning, or serve as an end all solution, but is a creative/effective additional benefit to an investor that needs whole life insurance.

Once again, it is imperative to consult a professional before considering this strategy and diligently reviewing policy options, terms, and fine print to fully evaluate all costs and conditions, which vary by provider.

## Final Expense Planning

For people generally more advanced in age, to purchase a "final expense" life insurance policy is a very effective and valuable investment. This type of policy is intended to cover the final funeral costs for the individual. At the time of writing this book, the average funeral in the US is between nine and thirteen thousand. That is a significant expense left behind for a family owner, so these policies are extremely useful in helping to make sure that none of those fees are passed on to leave a burden.

## Long Term Care Planning

Although this topic is not the best, investing in long term care can result in a world of mental and financial relief when it comes to paying for the health and living situation of the ones your love, especially if you're older. As stated in the earlier chapters of the book, investing in life insurance is a sure fire way to create generational wealth, and you have any concerns about yourself or someone you love being able to afford their living assistance/situation when the time comes, consulting an insurance agent and getting a LTC Rider put on your policy would be a worthwhile investment.

### HSA (Health Savings Account)

A hidden gem in the investing world, the health savings account (HSA), serves as the one of the most tax advantaged products on the market. For professionals that have a health insurance plan with a high deductible (whether it's through your job or personal) that has a deductible of $1500 for single people or $2700 for married couples, you are eligible to invest in a HSA. This HSA allows an investor to accumulate cash value to save for qualified medical expenses that exceed the coverage limits of their health insurance plan.

Contributions to this account for 2020 are limited to $3,500 for an individual and $7,100 for families and for 2021, $3,600 for an individual and $7,200 for families. All contributions to these accounts are tax deductible and can continue to rollover and accumulate year over year, creating a tax-sheltered savings vehicle for retirement. strategically investing into a product like this can serve as a great supplement to your current retirement. HSA's become eligible for penalty free withdrawal for any reason, starting at age 65, but will be subject to income tax unless utilized for qualified medical expenses.

# HOW TO WIN AT FINANCES

*"Your economic security does not lie in your job; it lies in your own power to produce—to think, to learn, to create, to adapt. That's true financial independence. It's not having wealth; it's having the power to produce wealth."* — **Stephen Covey**

The average American is a quarter of a million dollars in debt, between their home, car(s), credit cards, student loans, and any other things that they may take loans for. The country is quickly approaching a crisis as of September 22, 2020 the US national debt is $26,789,190,480,654 and rising with the average taxpayer debt right at $214,844. This debt is becoming too much to bear for many, and most people have not had the exposure or opportunity to learn this valuable financial knowledge that we shared with you to help them create a plan and eliminate that debt.

We truly believe that in order to WIN at finances, one must achieve financial freedom. For many people financial freedom carries different meanings, but for us, this means the ability to full fund your cost of living with strictly passive income. Meaning that you can afford to live and enjoy your life without having to go to work, meaning you can reallocate that time into your family, self-development, your health, and drastically increase your overall quality of life.

Financial freedom isn't necessarily about how much money you have, it's about how you make your money work for you. In order to do that it is imperative that you take the time to either develop your own strategy or truly consult a professional. From there it is up to you (& your professional if you choose to use one) to decide how to and what you choose to do to achieve that financial freedom.

Consulting with professionals can be a valuable asset to any investor looking to develop or advance their plan to financial freedom, whether they're a novice with low capital or a seasoned expert with established assets, the biggest factor is support and guidance. At the end of the day it is your life, your dream, and your money so when choosing someone to work for you, we highly recommend taking the time to vet their values and overall intention for you.

From the bottom of our hearts, we truly hope that each and every one of you take these products/strategies into account and use them to develop a plan for your own financial freedom. This book was meant to be extremely educational on many different topics, but the goal was to serve as a guide to inform and empower professionals in all stages of life to achieve financial freedom and shake the normality that many people truly believe they are stuck in.

We believe that every person reading this can utilize at least one of these strategies to start building wealth and that every person needs a financial plan. For anyone who has any questions, or would like to know what they can do starting today, we are always willing and eager to help. Please don't hesitate to visit our website www.winatfinances.com and reach out to us directly, so we can work together to help you WIN at Finances!

Made in the USA
Columbia, SC
12 November 2022

71042943R00033